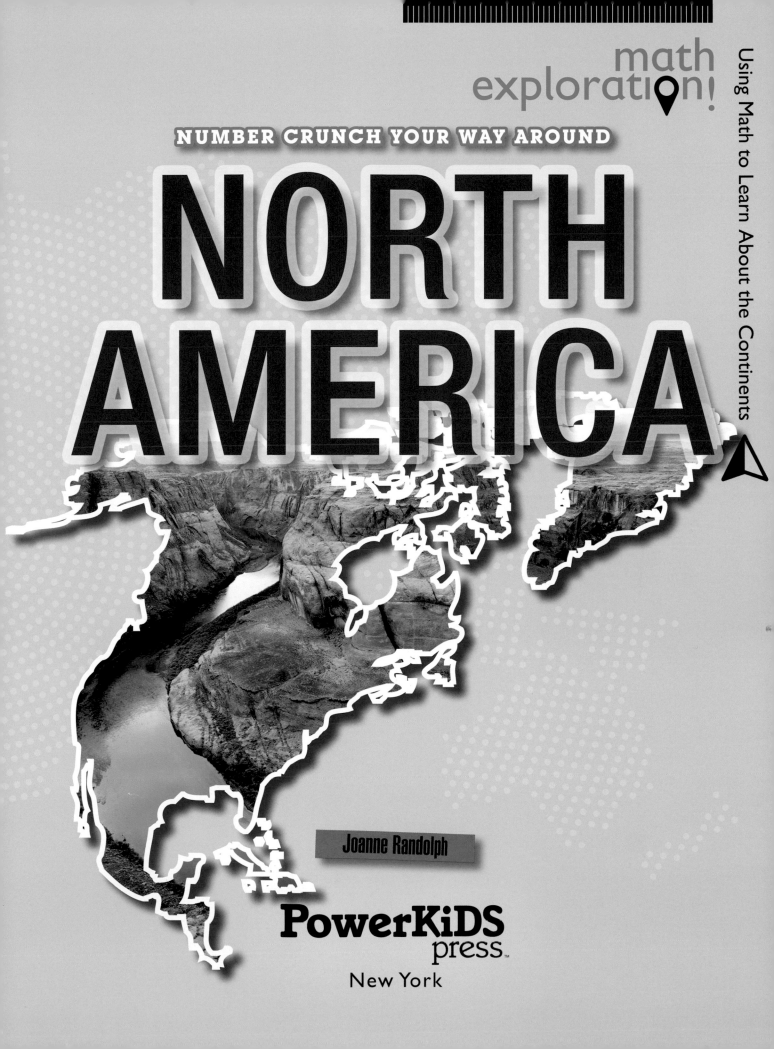

math
exploration!

Using Math to Learn About the Continents

NUMBER CRUNCH YOUR WAY AROUND

NORTH AMERICA

Joanne Randolph

PowerKiDS press™

New York

Published in 2016 by **The Rosen Publishing Group**
29 East 21st Street, New York, NY 10010

Produced for Rosen by Calcium

Editors for Calcium: Sarah Eason, Rosie Hankin, and Katie Dicker
Designer: Paul Myerscough

Art by Moloko88/Shutterstock

Photo credits: Cover: Dreamstime: Dan Breckwoldt (top); Shutterstock: Dennis W. Donohue (bottom),
Jessica Kirsh (back cover); Inside: Dreamstime: Dan Breckwoldt 28l; Shutterstock: American Spirit 11t,
Thorsteinn Asgeirsson 5t, Rudy Balasko 11br, Gerardo Borbolla 4b, Darren J. Bradley 21b, Dan Breckwoldt
7br, Jo Crebbin 8l, Critterbiz 22bl, Songquan Deng 5b, 29b, Anton Foltin 20r, 27c, Arto Hakola 20l, Holbox
26l, Jerry Horbert 13c, Jessicakirsh 16c, JoMo333 8br, Kan Khampanya 23t, Patryk Kosmider 18l, Jess Kraft
18r, LehaKoK 22-23b, Lemon Seven 16b, David Malik 10, MarkVanDykePhotography 9b, V. J. Matthew 9t,
Michal K. 25t, Outdoorsman 6c, 29t, Sean Pavone 13t, Mike Peters 24, Piotreknik 19b, Aleksei Potov 6t,
Rigucci 17br, Iriana Shiyan 5c, Siouxsnapp 13b, B. G. Smith 25br, Worachat Sodsri 27t, Somchaij 1, 15t,
SurangaSL 27b, Tusharkoley 14r.

Cataloging-in-Publication Data
Randolph, Joanne.
Number crunch your way around North America / by Joanne Randolph.
p. cm. — (Math exploration: using math to learn about the continents)
Includes index.
ISBN 978-1-4994-1037-2 (pbk.)
ISBN 978-1-4994-1035-8 (6 pack)
ISBN 978-1-4994-1034-1 (library binding)
1. North America — Juvenile literature. 2. Mathematics — Juvenile literature.
I. Randolph, Joanne. II. Title.
E38.5 R36 2016
970—d23

Manufactured in the United States of America
CPSIA Compliance Information: Batch WS15PK: For Further Information contact Rosen Publishing, New York, New York at 1-800-237-9932

Contents

North America

North America is the third-largest **continent** on Earth. It has an area of about 9.5 million square miles (24.6 million sq km). It has many different **geological** features, **ecosystems**, and plants and animals that make it a one-of-a-kind place. Get ready to begin a math exploration!

Arctic Ocean

Pacific Ocean

Atlantic Ocean

Mexico City

How to Use This Book

Look for the "Map-a-Stat" and "Do the Math" features and complete the math challenges. Then look at the answers on pages 28 and 29 to see if your calculations are correct.

More Than Meets the Eye

You may think of North America as being made up of Canada, the United States, and Mexico. These are the largest countries that share the continent, but there are 27 countries and territories in all. The countries in Central America, as well as many islands in the Caribbean Sea, are all part of the North American continent. **Greenland** is part of the North American continent, too, because it shares the same **tectonic plate**.

Map-a-Stat

The United States is 2,680 miles (4,312 km) wide, from the East Coast to the West Coast.

The North American continent has a population of around 530 million.

The population of the United States is around 318 million.

Mexico has more than 120 million people, and Canada has around 35 million people.

Greenland

New England

DO THE MATH!

Use the information in red in the Map-a-Stat box to figure out the following challenge. If the United States, Mexico, and Canada have the largest country populations in North America, what is the total population of the remaining countries of this continent? Here is the equation to help you solve the problem.

$$530,000,000 \text{ people} - (318,000,000 + 120,000,000 + 35,000,000) = ? \text{ people}$$

Complete the math challenge, then turn to pages 28–29 to see if your calculation is correct!

New York City

O, Canada!

Canada is North America's largest country by area. Canada is also the second-largest country in the world. It has 10 provinces and 3 territories. While Canada has its own government and **constitution**, it recognizes the Queen of England as its **monarch**.

North *vs.* South

Canada's capital is Ottawa, which is in Southern Ontario. Although Canada is larger than the United States, it has far fewer people. Around 75 percent of the Canadian people live in the southern part of the country, close to the border with the United States. This is because the northern parts of the country can be freezing cold and the land there is not **fertile**.

Lake Moraine is in Alberta, Canada.

Yukon Territory

Northwest Territory

Nunavut Territory

Newfoundland and Labrador

Quebec

Alberta

Manitoba

Prince Edward Island

British Columbia

Ontario

New Brunswick

territory

province

Saskatchewan

Nova Scotia

Map-a-Stat

At 5,525 miles (8,890 km) long, the border between the United States and Canada is the longest border between two countries.

Canada has the longest coastline in the world. It measures 125,556 miles (202,080 km).

Canada has 563 lakes that are larger than 39 square miles (100 sq km).

There are up to 25,000 polar bears in the world. Of that number, 15,000 live in Canada.

polar bears

DO THE MATH!

Use the information in red in the Map-a-Stat box to figure out the following challenge. How many polar bears live in places other than Canada? Here is the equation to help you solve the problem.

25,000 polar bears − 15,000 polar bears = ? polar bears

Complete the math challenge, then turn to pages 28–29 to see if your calculation is correct!

The city of Vancouver is on the West Coast of Canada, in British Columbia.

East Coast

Newfoundland and Labrador in Canada sit along the East coast of North America. New Brunswick, Nova Scotia, Prince Edward Island, and Quebec are along the East Coast, too. In the United States, the coast stretches from Maine to Florida. Maine and its Canadian neighbors have rocky shores and long, cold winters. As one heads south, the coasts become sandier and warmer. Beaches along North Carolina's Outer Banks and Florida are popular tourist stops, as are the islands in the Caribbean Sea.

Florida's Everglades

Florida is known for more than its beaches. It is also known for the Everglades, a giant **wetland** area that is home to hundreds of plant and animal **species**, including the American alligator. The Everglades are around 60 miles (97 km) wide and 100 miles (160 km) long.

A roseate spoonbill makes its home in Florida's Everglades.

Cape Charles, Virginia, sits on the Chesapeake Bay.

8

Map-a-Stat

The Appalachian Mountains stretch 1,500 miles (2,414 km) from Newfoundland all the way to Alabama.

The highest peak in the eastern United States is Mt. Mitchell in North Carolina, which is 6,684 feet (2,037 m) tall.

The Outer Banks of North Carolina are a 200-mile- (320 km) long string of **barrier islands**

and **peninsulas**. In 1903, Wilbur and Orville Wright took advantage of the windy conditions on the Outer Banks to work on building and flying the first successful airplanes.

The highest point in Florida is only 345 feet (105 m) above sea level. The average **elevation** of Florida is less than 50 feet (15 m) above sea level.

Prince Edward Island

Appalachian Mountains

DO THE MATH!

Use the information in red in the Map-a-Stat box to figure out the following challenge. Compare the highest peak on the East Coast with the highest point in Florida. How much taller is Mt. Mitchell? Here is the equation to help you solve the problem.

$6{,}684 \text{ feet} - 345 \text{ feet} = ? \text{ feet taller}$

Complete the math challenge, then turn to pages 28—29 to see if your calculation is correct!

9

The Midwestern United States

The Midwestern United States is made up of 12 states. These are Illinois, Indiana, Iowa, Kansas, Michigan, Minnesota, Missouri, Nebraska, North Dakota, Ohio, South Dakota, and Wisconsin. Six of the Midwestern States border the Great Lakes. The region has many large cities, such as Chicago and St. Louis, but is also known for its many farms.

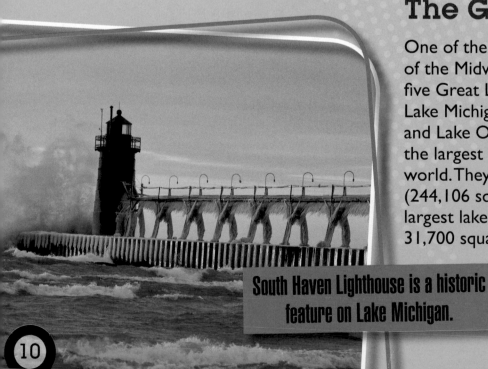

Lake Michigan

Lake Superior

Lake Huron

North Dakota

Minnesota

Wisconsin

South Dakota

Michigan

Nebraska

Iowa

Illinois · Indiana

Ohio

Lake Ontario

Kansas

Missouri

Lake Erie

The Great Lakes

One of the defining geographic features of the Midwest is the Great Lakes. The five Great Lakes are Lake Superior, Lake Michigan, Lake Huron, Lake Erie, and Lake Ontario. The Great Lakes are the largest freshwater system in the world. They cover 94,250 square miles (244,106 sq km). Lake Superior is the largest lake in the world, measuring 31,700 square miles (82,103 sq km).

South Haven Lighthouse is a historic feature on Lake Michigan.

Map-a-Stat

The Gateway Arch in St. Louis, Missouri, is the tallest man-made monument in the United States. The top of the arch stands 630 feet (192 m) tall.

4 out of 5 Great Lakes are part of the Midwest. The largest one is Lake Superior, which has a shore length of 1,729 miles (2,782 km).

The Mississippi River starts in the Midwest. It is 2,340 miles (3,765 km) long, and is an important **waterway** for transporting goods.

Chicago, Illinois, has more people than any other city in the Midwest.

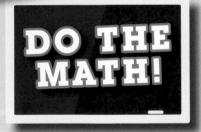

DO THE MATH!

Use the information in red in the Map-a-Stat box to figure out the following challenge. If you paddled around the shoreline of Lake Superior at a rate of 2 miles per hour, how long would it take you to get back to where you started? Round your answer. Here is the equation to help you solve the problem.

1,729 miles ÷ 2 miles per hour = ? hours

Complete the math challenge, then turn to pages 28—29 to see if your calculation is correct!

Gateway Arch, St. Louis

The Southern United States

The **South** is a region generally considered to be made up of 14 states: Virginia, West Virginia, North Carolina, South Carolina, Georgia, Florida, Tennessee, Kentucky, Mississippi, Alabama, Arkansas, Louisiana, Oklahoma, and Texas.

The **South** borders the **Atlantic Ocean** to the east and the **Gulf of Mexico** to the south. The **plains** and prairies of Texas and Oklahoma form the western border of the **South**. There are many lakes, rivers, coasts, caves, and mountains in the **South**.

Swamps, Rivers, and Mountains

The South is home to some of the world's most important wetlands, rivers, swamplands, and **bayous**. The Mississippi River ends in the south, flowing into the Gulf of Mexico at the port of New Orleans.

The South has some spectacular mountains. The Blue Ridge Mountains are part of the Appalachian Range and extend into North Carolina. They are known for their beautiful blue color when seen from a distance. The Great Smoky Mountains are also part of the Appalachian Range and are found in Tennessee and North Carolina.

These are cotton fields in the Southern United States.

West Virginia

Virginia

Kentucky

North Carolina

Tennessee

South Carolina

Oklahoma

Arkansas

Georgia

Mississippi

Alabama

Texas

Louisiana

Florida

Map-a-Stat

After Alaska, Texas is the second-largest state. The state is 261,232 square miles (420,412 sq km) in area.

Mammoth Cave in Kentucky is the longest known cave system in the world. There are 400 miles (644 km) of mapped passageways in the cave.

Nashville, Tennessee, is a well-known southern city.

Tourists like to visit the French Quarter in New Orleans, Louisiana.

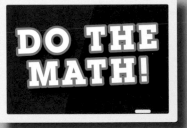

DO THE MATH!

Use the information in red in the Map-a-Stat box to figure out the following challenge. If you were to walk at a speed of 2 miles per hour, how many hours would it take you to walk the length of the Mammoth Cave and back again? Here is the equation to help you solve the problem.

(400 miles ÷ 2 miles per hour) x 2 = ? hours

Complete the math challenge, then turn to pages 28—29 to see if your calculation is correct!

The Southwestern United States

The **Southwest** is generally considered to be made up of five states: Arizona, New Mexico, Colorado, Utah, and Nevada. The place where Colorado, Utah, Arizona, and New Mexico meet is called the Four Corners. Sometimes, California, Texas, and Oklahoma are included in the Southwest, but only parts of these states are in the geographic Southwest.

Hot and Dry

The Southwest has an **arid climate**. This means that there is little rainfall or vegetation there. The Southwest has rivers, mountains, deserts, **mesas**, and some prairies. There are also canyons in the region, such as the Grand Canyon. The Southwest is famous for some of its beautiful rock formations, such as the arches at Arches National Park in Utah. Carlsbad Caverns is a system of more than 300 underground caves in New Mexico.

Double Arch is a rock formation found in Arches National Park.

Nevada

Utah

Colorado

Arizona

New Mexico

Map-a-Stat

Carlsbad Caverns is the remains of a reef that was part of an inland sea, more than 250 million years ago.

Prairie dogs, which live in the Southwestern United States, among other places, are known for digging burrows up to 108 feet (33 m) long.

Chaco Canyon in New Mexico has the ruins of a huge settlement built by **native people** more than 1,000 years ago. One of the structures there is guessed to have taken 5,000 trees and 50 million stone blocks to build!

Arches National Park in Utah has more than 2,000 natural stone arches. In order to be considered an arch, an opening between the stones must be at least 3 feet (1 m). Some arches are more than 300 feet (91 m) across.

DO THE MATH!

Use the information in red in the Map-a-Stat box to figure out the following challenge. What is the difference in width between the largest arches and the smallest? Here is the equation to help you solve the problem.

$$300 \text{ feet} - 3 \text{ feet} = ? \text{ feet}$$

Complete the math challenge, then turn to pages 28—29 to see if your calculation is correct!

West Coast

The West Coast of North America is made up of the states of California, Oregon, and Washington, and the Canadian province of British Columbia. Its eastern border is formed by the Sierra Nevada mountain range, the Cascade Range, and the Mojave Desert. The West Coast also has some fertile regions, including the Puget Sound area in Washington, the Willamette Valley in Oregon, and the Central Valley in California.

The Golden Gate Bridge, in San Francisco, is 6,450 feet (1,966 m) long.

Washington

Oregon

California

Oregon's climate makes it well suited to vineyards.

Wilderness and Cities

The Sierra Nevada, which is 250 miles (400 km) long and about 70 miles (112 km) wide, forms part of the eastern border of California. This range has many famous national forests and wilderness areas, such as Yosemite, Sequoia National Park, and Lake Tahoe. The West Coast has many large cities, too. These include San Francisco, San Diego, and Los Angeles in California; Portland, Oregon; Seattle, Washington; and Vancover, British Columbia.

Map-a-Stat

Death Valley, in California, is the hottest and lowest place in North America. It is 282 feet (86 m) below sea level. The Dead Sea, between Israel and Jordan, is the lowest place on Earth at 1,371 feet (418 m) below sea level.

The driving distance from San Diego to Los Angeles is 125 miles (201 km). It is another 381 miles (613 km) to drive from Los Angeles to San Francisco.

The West Coast has 33 national forests and huge areas of protected wilderness.

Seattle's Space Needle has a rotating restaurant and an observation deck from which to take in the city views. Including its antenna, the building is 605 feet (184 m) tall.

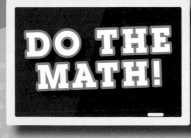

DO THE MATH!

Use the information in red in the Map-a-Stat box to figure out the following challenge. If you wanted to drive from San Diego to San Francisco with a stop in Los Angeles, how many miles would you need to drive? Here is the equation to help you solve the problem.

125 miles + 381 miles = ? miles

Complete the math challenge, then turn to pages 28–29 to see if your calculation is correct!

Space Needle, Seattle

Mexico

Mexico covers nearly 760,000 square miles (1,968,400 sq km). It is made up of 31 states and a capital district. More than 120 million people make their home in Mexico. Some 200,000 species of plants and animals make their home there, too. Mexico has mountain ranges, many rivers, and around 92,655 square miles (240,000 sq km) of protected natural areas.

Mexico

The Caribbean Sea off Mexico's coast is home to many kinds of turtles.

Mexico City is Mexico's capital.

Rich in History

Mexico has 32 **World Heritage Sites**, including the Mayan ruins at Chichen Itza. Many of these historic sites are ruins from the ancient people who ruled in Mexico long ago, such as the Olmec, Toltec, Maya, and Aztecs. Other sites remember the influence of the Spanish who came and **conquered** the ancient empires. Some of these sites simply **preserve** some of Mexico's natural beauty, such as the Gulf of California and the whale **sanctuary** off El Vizcaino.

Kukulkan Pyramid, Chichen Itza

Map-a-Stat

Chichen Itza is a city that was built by the Mayan civilization around 1,000 years ago. El Castillo is the central temple of the city. Each side of the pyramid has a staircase with 91 steps. The pyramid is 78 feet (24 m) tall.

Mexico is 1 of around 17 countries that are considered to be **megadiverse**. This means they are home to many different kinds of plants and animals. Mexico has around 200,000 known species. It has the second-highest number of **reptiles** in the world, with 804 species, and the third-highest number of **mammals**, with 535 species. It has 361 known **amphibian** species. It also has more than 23,424 different kinds of **nonvascular** plants!

The Large Millimeter Telescope in Mexico is the largest of its kind and was built to see areas in space that have a lot of dust. It has a diameter of 164 feet (50 m).

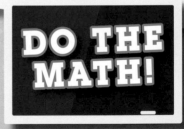

DO THE MATH!

Use the information in red in the Map-a-Stat box to figure out the following challenge. If you were to climb El Castillo at a rate of 1 step per second, how many minutes would it take you to reach the top of the temple? Round your answer. Use this equation to help you solve the problem.

(91 steps ÷ 1 step per second) ÷ 60 seconds = ? minutes

Complete the math challenge, then turn to pages 28—29 to see if your calculation is correct!

Deserts

North America has four main deserts. These are the **Chihuahuan Desert,** the **Great Basin Desert,** the **Mojave Desert,** and the **Sonoran Desert.** Most of these deserts are hot deserts, like the ones most of us think of when we imagine a desert. The Great Basin is considered a cold desert, though, because of its cooler temperatures and the kinds of plants and animals that live there.

Mojave Desert

Sonoran Desert

Great Basin Desert

Chihuahuan Desert

Saguaro cactuses are found only in the Sonoran Desert.

This is a Great Basin collared lizard.

Desert Animals

Deserts are difficult places in which to live, but many animals and plants find them the perfect place to call home. Desert animals have **adapted** to life in these dry places. Jackrabbits have giant ears that help them cool off. Desert tortoises spend their days inside burrows underground, and only come out during the cooler nights. Some animals get all the water they need from the plants they eat, such as cactuses.

Map-a-Stat

The Chihuahuan Desert covers more than 175,000 square miles (453,250 sq km) of the United States and Mexico. Most of the desert gets less than 10 inches (25 cm) of rain each year.

The Great Basin is the largest US desert. It sits between the Sierra Nevada range and the Rocky Mountains. It receives between 7–12 inches (18–30 cm) of rain each year.

The Mojave Desert has at least 200 kinds of plants and animals that are not found in neighboring deserts. It averages less than 6 inches (15 cm) of rain each year.

The Sonoran Desert is the hottest desert in North America. However, some areas get rain twice a year, which allows a larger variety of plants and animals to do well there. On average, this desert gets less than 15 inches (38 cm) of rain each year.

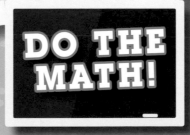

DO THE MATH!

Use the information in red in the Map-a-Stat box to figure out the following challenge. Make a bar graph showing the average precipitation, or rainfall, in each desert every year. Which desert gets the least precipitation? You can use this chart to help you figure out the answer, too.

Desert	Precipitation (avg.)
Chihuahuan	10 inches or less
Great Basin	12 inches or less
Mojave	6 inches or less
Sonoran	15 inches or less

Valley of Fire, Mojave Desert

Complete the math challenge, then turn to pages 28–29 to see if your calculation is correct!

Forests

The United States has 154 national forests, which are protected forest areas. Almost 50 percent of Canada's land is covered by forests. Mexico also has a lot of forested land, including dry forests, pine and oak forests, and the Lacandón Rain Forest. Many of Mexico's forests cover its numerous mountain ranges.

Redwood Forests

California and southwestern Oregon are home to the tallest tree species on Earth, the coast redwood. Redwood forests once covered 3,125 square miles (8,094 sq km) of the Californian coast. However, logging has destroyed around 95 percent of these forests. Today, national parks protect the remaining coast redwoods.

Black bears make their homes in forests across North America.

Giant sequoias are trees that can grow so large it can take several people to reach around their trunks.

Hoh Forest

Map-a-Stat

Hoh Forest, in Washington State, receives up to 170 inches (432 cm) of rain each year. That is up to 14 feet (4.27 m) of rain!

Canada's forests make up 10 percent of the world's forests. Nearly 70 percent of Canadian forests are coniferous, which means they are evergreen, cone-bearing trees.

Around 0.5 percent of Mexico's forests are cut down each year. Much of this land is turned into pastureland for cattle.

Coast redwoods can grow to be 300 feet (91 m) tall and many are 30 feet (9 m) around. The oldest redwood lived for about 2,200 years, and there are many still living that are older than 600 years.

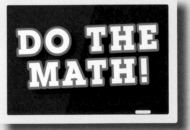

DO THE MATH!

Use the information in red in the Map-a-Stat box and the desert rainfall chart on page 21 to figure out the following challenge. How much more rain does the Hoh Forest receive than all the North American deserts added together? Here is the equation to help you solve the problem.

$$170 \text{ inches} - (10 + 12 + 6 + 15)$$
$$= ? \text{ more inches of rain}$$

Complete the math challenge, then turn to pages 28–29 to see if your calculation is correct!

Mountains

There are plenty of mountain ranges in North America with impressive peaks. Each of the three largest countries in North America has several peaks that are more than 15,000 feet (4,572 m) tall. The three tallest peaks on the continent are Denali, or Mt. McKinley, in Alaska, Mt. Logan in Canada, and Volcán Citlaltépetl in Mexico.

The Rocky Mountains

The Rocky Mountains, also called the Rockies, stretch from Canada to New Mexico. They were formed more than 35 million years ago. The highest peak in the Rockies is Mt. Elbert in Colorado. It stands at 14,433 feet (4,399 m) tall. The Rockies are home to bighorn sheep, moose, elk, deer, bears, coyotes, and more. There are many forests in the range, as well.

Mt. Logan

Denali

The Rocky Mountains

Volcán Citlaltépetl

The Aspen Highlands in Aspen, Colorado, are a top skiing destination.

24

Map-a-Stat

Of the top 200 tallest mountains in North America, 159 are in the United States, 31 in Canada, and there are 10 in Mexico. Many of the tallest US peaks are found in Alaska.

Alaska's Denali is 20,320 feet (6,194 m) tall. Mt. Logan, in Canada's Yukon Territory, is 19,551 feet (5,959 m) tall and Volcán Citlaltépetl in Mexico is 18,406 feet (5,610 m) tall.

North America's top 3 peaks do not even make the top 100 in the list of the world's highest peaks. The tallest mountain on Earth is Mt. Everest at 29,035 feet (8,850 m). The 100th tallest in the world is Mt. Karjiang, in Tibet, which measures 23,691 feet (7,221 m) tall.

The Rocky Mountains stretch 3,000 miles (4,828 km) from northern British Columbia in Canada all the way down to New Mexico.

Denali is the tallest peak in North America.

Bighorn sheep live in the Rocky Mountains.

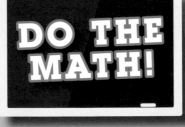

DO THE MATH!

Use the information in red in the Map-a-Stat box to figure out the following challenge. How much taller is Mt. Everest than Denali? How much taller is the 100th tallest mountain in the world than Denali? Here are the equations to help you solve the problem.

29,035 feet − 20,320 feet = ? feet
23,691 feet − 20,320 feet = ? feet

Complete the math challenge, then turn to pages 28—29 to see if your calculation is correct!

From Sea to Shining Sea

North America is a beautiful continent. Its East Coast sits on the Atlantic Ocean and its West Coast borders the Pacific. In between, there are many different ecosystems, climates, and geographic features. There are huge cities, tiny towns, and vast wildernesses.

These colorful boats rest on an island beach off the coast of Mexico.

Banff National Park

Grand Canyon National Park

New York City

Mexico City

Much to Explore

Amazing national parks, such as the Grand Canyon National Park in Arizona and the Banff National Park in Alberta, Canada, remind us what the continent might have been like before European settlers arrived. In contrast, beautiful, modern cities, such as Mexico City and New York City, remind us how far we have come. North America is certainly worth exploring!

Miami, Florida

Mission Santa Barbara

Northern Lights

Map-a-Stat

Canada has many islands. Ellesmere Island is Canada's northernmost point. The island is the tenth-largest island in the world, yet, due to its climate, only 146 people live there.

Mexico City is the largest city in North America, with around 8.8 million people. New York City has the second-largest population, with 8.4 million people.

The Grand Canyon is more than 6,000 feet (1,800 m) deep and 18 miles (29 km) wide.

Mexico has more than 30 UNESCO World Heritage Sites, which makes it a popular place to visit. UNESCO works to identify and keep safe important **cultural**, natural, and historical places in the world.

DO THE MATH!

Use the information in red in the Map-a-Stat box to figure out the following challenge. How many more people live in Mexico City than live in New York City? Here is the equation to help you solve the problem.

8,800,000 people –
8,400,000 people = ? people

Complete the math challenge, then turn to pages 28—29 to see if your calculation is correct!

Math Challenge Answers

You have made it through the math exploration! How did your math skills measure up? Check your answers below.

Page 5

530,000,000 people – (318,000,000 + 120,000,000 + 35,000,000) = 57,000,000 people

Page 7

25,000 polar bears – 15,000 polar bears = 10,000 polar bears

Page 9

6,684 feet – 345 feet = 6,339 feet taller

Page 11

1,729 miles ÷ 2 miles per hour = 865 hours

Page 13

(400 miles ÷ 2 miles per hour) × 2 = 400 hours

Page 15

300 feet – 3 feet = 297 feet

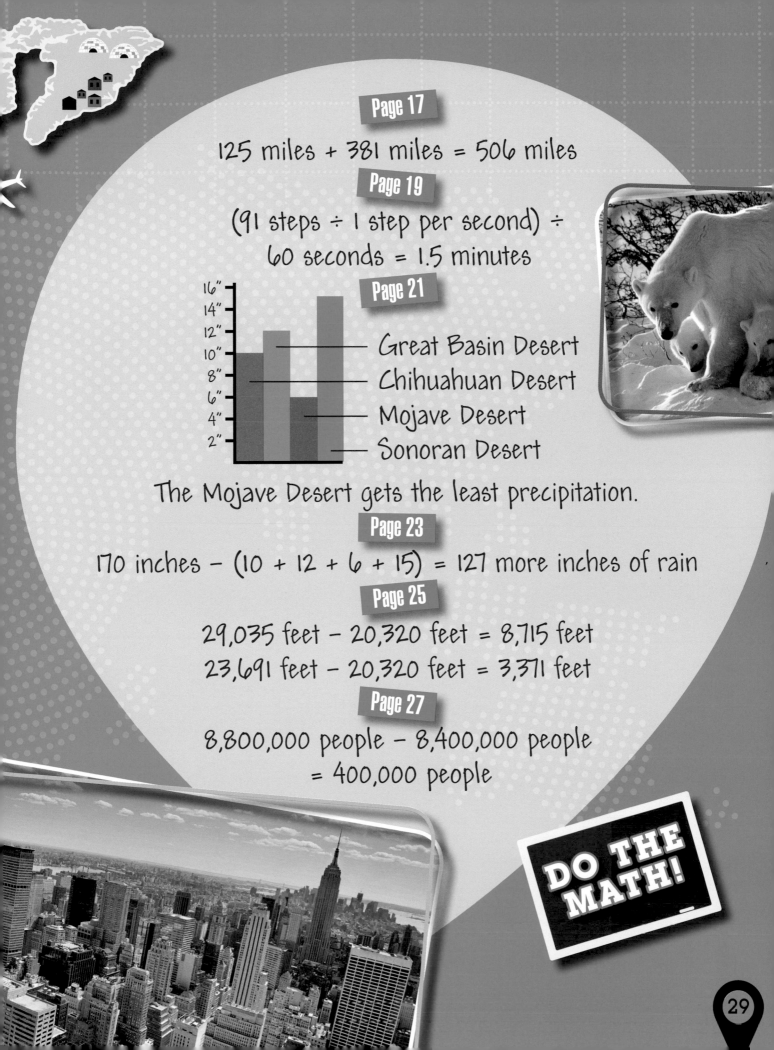

Page 17

125 miles + 381 miles = 506 miles

Page 19

(91 steps ÷ 1 step per second) ÷
60 seconds = 1.5 minutes

Page 21

16"
14"
12"
10"
8"
6"
4"
2"

Great Basin Desert
Chihuahuan Desert
Mojave Desert
Sonoran Desert

The Mojave Desert gets the least precipitation.

Page 23

170 inches − (10 + 12 + 6 + 15) = 127 more inches of rain

Page 25

29,035 feet − 20,320 feet = 8,715 feet
23,691 feet − 20,320 feet = 3,371 feet

Page 27

8,800,000 people − 8,400,000 people
= 400,000 people

DO THE MATH!

Glossary

adapted Changed in order to survive.

amphibian A cold-blooded animal that spends part of its life in water and part on land.

arid climate Very hot, dry weather.

barrier islands Islands that are found near the coast and that form a barrier between the coast and the ocean.

bayous Slow-moving bodies of water that flow out of lakes or rivers in the Southern United States.

cactuses Plants with tough, leathery stems or leaves that are covered with spines. Cactuses can survive in very dry places, such as deserts.

conquered Overcame.

constitution The basic rules by which a country or a state is governed.

continent One of Earth's seven large landmasses.

cultural The type of music, art, literature, and customs of a people.

ecosystems The interconnected living things, such as animals and plants, and the nonliving things, such as air and water, in one place.

elevation The height above sea level of an object or area.

fertile Describes ground that is rich and able to produce crops and other plants.

geological Relating to Earth's rocks and minerals.

Greenland A large, very cold island in northern North America.

mammals Animals that have warm blood and often fur. Most mammals give birth to live young and feed their babies with milk from their bodies.

megadiverse Having a high percentage of Earth's plant and animal species.

mesas High landforms with steep sides and flat tops.

monarch A king or queen.

native people People who are born in a place and whose ancestors lived there.

nonvascular Not having a vascular system, which is a series of veins that transport fluid around the body.

peninsulas Areas of land that are surrounded on three sides by ocean.

plains Large, flat areas of land often covered in grasses.

preserve To keep something from being lost or from going bad.

reptiles Animals that have scales covering their bodies and that use the sun to control their body temperature.

sanctuary A place where people or animals are kept safe.

species A single kind of living thing. All people are one species.

tectonic plate A moving piece of Earth's crust, or the top layer of Earth.

waterway A stretch of water that is used to transport goods by boat or ship.

wetland Low-lying area, such as a marsh or swamp, where the ground is saturated with water.

World Heritage Sites Places in the world that are protected for their beauty or importance.

Further Reading

Books

Cordey, Huw. *North America: A World in One Continent.* Philadelphia, PA: Running Press, 2013.

Gibson, Karen Bush. *North America* (The Seven Continents). Mankato, MN: Capstone Press, 2006.

Hirsch, Rebecca. *North America* (Rookie Read-About Geography). New York, NY: Scholastic, 2012.

Koponen, Libby. *North America* (True Books: Geography). Danbury, CT: Children's Press, 2009.

National Geographic Kids United States Atlas. Des Moines, IA: National Geographic Kids, 2012.

Websites

Due to the changing nature of Internet links, PowerKids Press has developed an online list of websites related to the subject of this book. This site is updated regularly. Please use this link to access the list:
www.powerkidslinks.com/me/namer

Index